The Really Wild Life of Frogs™

WOOD FROGS

DOUG WECHSLER

THE ACADEMY OF NATURAL SCIENCES

The Rosen Publishing Group's
PowerKids Press™
New York

An dr Familie Nüscheler, wo in dr frielig vo mi läbe e platz in där ihre Teich hät gäh

About the Author
Wildlife biologist, ornithologist, and photographer Doug Wechsler has studied birds, snakes, frogs, and other wildlife around the world. Doug Wechsler works at The Academy of Natural Sciences of Philadelphia, a natural history museum. As part of his job, he travels to the rain forest and remote parts of the world to take pictures of birds. He has taken part in expeditions to Ecuador, the Philippines, Borneo, Cuba, Cameroon, and many other countries.

Published in 2002 by The Rosen Publishing Group, Inc.
29 East 21st Street, New York, NY 10010

Copyright © 2002 by The Rosen Publishing Group, Inc.

First Edition

Book Design: Michael de Guzman, Michael Donnellan, Emily Muschinske
Project Editor: Kathy Campbell

Photo Credits: All photos © Doug Wechsler

Wechsler, Doug.
   Wood frogs / Doug Wechsler. —1st ed.
      p. cm. — (The really wild life of frogs)
   ISBN 0–8239–5854–X (lib. bdg.)
  1. Wood frog—Juvenile literature. [1. Wood frog. 2. Frogs.] I. Title
   QL668.E27 W43 2002
   597.8'9—dc21

                                                              00–012296

Manufactured in the United States of America

CONTENTS

WHO IS THAT MASKED FROG?

It wears a robber mask. It is the color of dead leaves. It has webbed feet. What is it? It is a wood frog. This frog is truly a frog of the woods. A wood frog is shaped like the frogs we see in ponds. It swims well, but it visits water only to breed or to mate and lay eggs. Most of the time, wood frogs live in the woods.

Wood frogs live farther north than any other frog in North America. You can find them in Alaska, north of the **Arctic Circle**. They live in Canada, most of the eastern United States, and in some parts of the West. No other frog in North America can be found from so far north to so far south or as far from east to west as the wood frog.

Adult wood frogs range in size from 1 ⅜ inches (3.5 cm) to 2 ¾ inches (7 cm).

FIRST SIGN OF SPRING

The call of the wood frog announces the end of winter. The first warm days of the year bring wood frogs out of the woods. They go to the ponds where they breed. In the southern United States, the time to breed is in January and February. In the North, wood frogs hop to the pond in April, May, or June. They are usually the first **species** of frog to call. Males make a soft, quacking noise that sounds a little like a duck's quack. To make the noise, the male forces air from his lungs into his **vocal sacs**. The sacs are like two small balloons on the sides of the body behind the jaws. On the way, the air shakes the **vocal cords**, which make the sound.

The wood frog's calls, or songs, tell other wood frogs, "This is the place to breed."

DOUG SAYS
TO SEE WOOD FROGS WITHOUT SCARING THEM, IT IS BEST TO GO TO THE POND AT NIGHT WITH A FLASHLIGHT.

TO THE POND

The calls soon draw other wood frogs to the same corner of the pond. Within a few hours, 100 males are quacking away. They will quack day and night until all the females have come and gone.

One day the pond is quiet. Boom! The next day it is noisy with as many as 100 frogs. In the pond, each male swims back and forth searching for females. When one arrives, a male frog grabs her. He rides on her back until she is ready to lay eggs. In a couple of days, all the eggs are laid and breeding is done. **Amphibians** that breed like this are called **explosive breeders**. This is because breeding happens so quickly.

Like an explosion, wood frog breeding happens suddenly. There is lots of action and then it ends quickly.

EGGS BY THE THOUSANDS

Wood frogs lay their eggs in clusters, or clumps. A single cluster can have up to 2,500 eggs. As the female lays the eggs, the male releases **sperm** to **fertilize** them. Fertilized eggs can grow into tadpoles.

The eggs come out covered with a very thin layer of jelly. Water quickly soaks into the jelly to make it expand. The egg cluster will grow in hours from the size of a large marble to almost the size of a tennis ball. The jelly makes it harder for animals to eat the eggs.

After the eggs are laid, the male lets go of the female. Soon she leaves the pond. She has spent only a few hours in the water. She will not return again until next year.

The male holds onto the female and fertilizes the eggs as she lays them.

DOUG SAYS

IF YOU WANT TO SEE WOOD FROGS LAY EGGS, YOU HAVE TO BE READY TO GO TO THE POND AS SOON AS THE CALLING STARTS.

EGGS IN JELLY

The frogs lay nearly all of the eggs in the same corner of the pond. Soon the clusters expand to touch one another. Being one huge mass of jelly helps to hold in the warmth of the sun. The jelly around the eggs turns green as time goes on. **Microscopic** green plants called **algae** are growing inside the jelly. Inside each egg is a little, round, black **embryo**. It would not even fill an "o" on this page. The embryo will become a tadpole. The embryo changes shape as it grows. It gets longer and skinnier. After three weeks, the embryo has become a tadpole. It is ready to hatch. When the tadpole wriggles out of the egg, it is only ¼ inch (6 mm) long.

The algae do not harm the eggs, and they may even help them. These tiny plants give off oxygen, which the eggs need to live.

FROM POLLYWOG TO FROG

You could call tadpoles feeding machines. They spend most of their time eating. Their ponds sometimes dry up by early summer, so the tadpoles must grow fast. They scrape food from leaves and other surfaces under water. Their favorite food is algae.

The inside of a tadpole is mostly guts. Plants are hard to digest. Animals that eat plants need a long gut to break down their food. When the food is digested, the body uses it to grow. Being mostly guts helps tadpoles to grow quickly.

A wood frog tadpole grows for about nine weeks and then changes into a frog. As soon as its arms and legs grow out, the tadpole's tail starts to shrink.

This tadpole does not have arms or legs yet. It can swim only by using its tail like a fish.

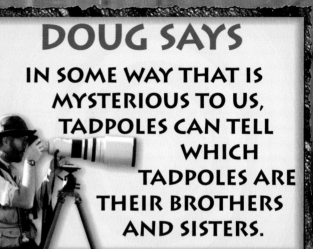

DOUG SAYS

IN SOME WAY THAT IS MYSTERIOUS TO US, TADPOLES CAN TELL WHICH TADPOLES ARE THEIR BROTHERS AND SISTERS.

TO THE WOODS

Once the young frog's tail shrinks, the frog leaves the pond. The little wood frog enters the woods, where it will spend most of its life. Wood frogs like moist woods. They cannot live in dry conditions. Wood frogs find their food on the forest floor. They eat many kinds of small insects. Beetles, caterpillars, and crickets are some of the wood frog's favorite foods.

The shade in the forest keeps the temperature cooler. There are plenty of places to hide on the forest floor. A quick hop carries the frog beneath a root. Leaves provide protection when it is cold. Many enemies also lurk in the woods. Garter snakes, raccoons, and red-shouldered hawks are just a few of the animals that eat wood frogs.

Wood frogs take up water through their skin from wet ground or plants.

"FROGSICLES"

In winter it is too cold for frogs to move. Frogs must **hibernate**, or become inactive. Many other frogs, such as bullfrogs and leopard frogs, go underwater to the bottom of a pond where it never freezes. Wood frogs stay in their forest homes. They dig down into the leaves or beneath a log. They rest through winter.

Wood frogs have a special way to prepare for cold weather. They build up lots of sugar in their blood. The sugar makes the blood thick, like syrup. This keeps important parts of the frog's body from freezing. The wood frog can **survive** temperatures as low as 19 degrees Fahrenheit (–7° C). Much of the frog's body freezes. Their heart and breathing both stop.

When winter ends and the weather warms up, wood frogs thaw out and soon are ready to head for the pond to breed again.

Wood frogs lay their eggs in a variety of ponds, but **vernal pools** are the safest. A vernal pool is a special kind of pond. It dries up almost every summer. It has no stream feeding it. It has no fish. Fish are the enemies of frogs. Fish cannot survive in vernal pools because these pools go dry. If fish could survive in them, they would gobble up the wood frogs' eggs.

Vernal pools are very important to other kinds of frogs. Vernal pools are also home to salamanders, insects, and fairy shrimp. Wood frogs sometimes breed in other types of ponds, streams, and ditches. Most of these places have no fish in them. Most of them also dry out in summer.

Many kinds of animals live only in vernal pools like this one. This pool is shown in June, when it is full of water.

SAVING PLACES FOR WOOD FROGS

Most people do not realize how important vernal pools are. The pools are small and shallow. They may be hidden in the woods. For parts of the year, they have no water. It takes a bulldozer only a few minutes to fill one. In the state of Massachusetts, there is a law protecting vernal pools. First someone must prove that the pool is a vernal pool. Finding eggs and **larvae** of wood frogs or mole salamanders is good proof. Then the pond can be **registered** with the government as a vernal pool.

Many kids have worked to register vernal pools for protection. They have saved places for wood frogs. Other states need laws like this, too.

GLOSSARY

algae (AL-jee) Plants without roots or stems that usually live in the water.

amphibians (am-FIH-bee-unz) Animals that are able to live both on land and in the water.

Arctic Circle (ARK-tic SUR-kul) The imaginary circle around the northern part of Earth. It marks off the coldest part of the northern half of the world.

embryo (EM-bree-oh) The form of a plant or an animal as it grows before birth.

explosive breeders (ik-SPLOH-siv BREE-derz) Animals that get together in large numbers to mate and lay eggs in a very short period of time.

fertilize (FUR-til-iyz) To introduce male reproductive cells to the female cells in order to begin development and growth.

hibernate (HY-bur-nate) To spend the winter sleeping or resting.

larvae (LAR-vee) The plural form of larva: the early life stage of certain animals that differs greatly from the adult stage.

microscopic (my-kreh-SCAH-pik) Very small.

registered (REH-jeh-stird) When something has been listed at a special office.

species (SPEE-sheez) Groups of animals or plants that are very much alike.

sperm (SPERM) A special male cell that, if joined with a female egg, can develop into offspring.

survive (sur-VYV) To live longer than; to stay alive.

vernal pools (VUR-nul POOLZ) Small ponds that have water only part of the year, have no stream flowing in, and have no fish.

vocal cords (VOH-kul KORDZ) Thin strands in the voice box that make sound when air rushes through them.

vocal sacs (VOH-kul SAX) Thin, balloonlike pockets near the mouth of a frog that fill with air and change the sound when the frog calls.

INDEX

WEB SITES

To learn more about wood frogs, check out these Web sites:
http://animaldiversity.ummz.umich.edu/accounts/rana/r._sylvatica
http://earth.simmons.edu/vernal/pool/inf_wf.htm